方仙延年法
揉腹卻病延年

Immortal Fang's Longevity Qigong

Rubbing the Abdomen
to Prevent Illness and Prolong Life

Translated by Franklin Fick

Shen Long Publishing
shenlongpub.com

Shen Long Publishing
shenlongpub.com

Originally Published 1723

English Translation Copyright © 2018 by Franklin Fick.
All Rights Reserved.

Disclaimer
This book is intended for informational purposes only. The author (s), translator (s), and publisher of this book disclaim all responsibility for any liability, loss, injury, or risk, personal or otherwise, which is incurred as a consequence, directly or indirectly from reading and or following the instructions contained herein.

Please consult your physician before starting any exercise program.

Table of Contents

Translator's Introduction

I have the habit of searching used book stores and online sites for old books. While browsing one day, I found an old hand bound book about preventing illness and prolonging life. Intrigued by the preview the bookseller provided, I decided to purchase it.

When I received the book, I found that the hand bound copy included information from several different sources. One section illustrated a set of exercises that I recognized as being part of the system that one of my late teachers taught.

After doing some research, I found that the section of the book I was interested in was reprinted in 1984 and that it seemed to be a lot longer then what was included in the hand bound copy that I had. Naturally, I ordered a copy of this reprint. But, I found that the additional length of the 1984 reprint was actually a second book about Traditional Chinese Medicine (Wan Bing Hui Chun – Return of Spring for all Diseases) that was reprinted along with the book I was interested in.

What you have in your hands, is a translation of a book originally published in 1723 detailing Daoist Fang's method of Rubbing the Abdomen to Prevent Illness and Prolong Life.

This book has gone through a series of reprints over the years. Each time it has been made available, the story behind the reprint is strikingly similar. Somebody received a copy of the book from a friend, tried the exercises, and found that they had good results, then decided to make the information available to a wider audience by publishing it.

- It was originally published in 1723 by Song Xinru. (see Original Introduction and Continued Introduction)
- It was republished by Zhu Tianfu in 1860. He received a copy from Mr. Ran's collection. He used the exercises to improve his health. He made the information available and other people also received good results from the exercises. (see the Continued Introduction)
- It was republished again in 1925 by Lu Yisu. Lu was originally a Xingyi Quan student of Jin Yunting. He received the book from his friend and coworker Wu Heshou (who received it from his friend and coworker Government Offical Peng). Lu Yisu slightly organized and revised the text with the help of his teacher Jin Yunting and he republished it because no original copies still existed. (see Introduction and Postscript)

This method of Rubbing the Abdomen to Prevent Illness and Prolong Life as passed on by Daoist Fang consists of nine exercises. Exercises 1 through 8 should be done in sequence and repeated for a number of repetitions. Then you close the set with exercise 9.

When you first start, you should do 3 repetitions (of exercises 1 through 8). Then 3 days later you should do 5 repetitions. Then 3 days later you should do 7 repetitions.

According to the text, 7 repetitions is the complete practice and the set should be done at least twice a day, morning and night.

The set can be done standing up or laying down. And, "No matter if you are a man or a woman, it is suitable for all people, except for pregnant women who are forbidden (to practice)."

Because of my years of experience as a practitioner of Traditional Chinese Medicine, as a Qigong practitioner, and as a Qigong teacher, I have first hand experience and have seen that simple exercises, like the ones presented in this book, can have tremendous positive results for people who take the time to practice them. As I present the English language translation of this book in 2018, my hope is similar to those that came before me in reprinting this volume, namely to make this available to a wider audience so that more people can benefit from the content.

Franklin Fick, October 31st 2018, Taipei Taiwan

Introduction

My body was formerly frail. I had lung disease. Sometimes it would stop and sometimes it would act up. I exhausted all options with doctors and medicines. I was aware that Xingyi Quan can cure this disease and I thought about practicing it. It just so happened that, Mr. Jin Yunting traveled south from the big city and he is an expert in this practice. We discussed this and practiced for a few years. My disease reduced and disappeared.
I hoped to cure those who have the same disease as me, so I discussed with Mr. Jin about publishing his secret scroll on Xingyi Quan that he collected. I already paid the DaDong (Great East) Bookstore to print the manual with the explanation and picture, therefore it sounded appropriate to ask.

In Wu Jin, Government Official Peng and I were good at Yang Sheng (Nourishing Life), white hair but a ruddy complexion and a zesty demeanor. This Spring (return of good health or youth) is the essence of this book. This year I am 76 years old. My body is still healthy. I practiced this method for several decades without stop.

He had the same aspirations (as me). He gave me this book. I opened and read it once. It is mostly methods of getting rid of disease and it is not in the same category as Xingyi Quan. It is about the mechanism of generation or birthing (the endless cosmic force of creation). The changes are miraculous. It uses movement to transform stillness and uses stillness to facilitate movement. Compared to Xingyi Quan, it is more easy and comfortable.

This book was written in Yongzheng (1723-1735) and continued (to be circulated) in Xianfeng (1851-1861). Today none of the original versions exist, scattered like (the incident at) Guangling. Because of this, Mr Jin and I examined it in detail, slightly revised it, and printed it for people with a common interest. As for the 10 methods I practiced, it is recorded in detail and explained with pictures so I will not repeat it here.

First half of the second winter month, year Yi Chou (1925)
Basic outline by Lu Yisu, in the Capital of Baxian

Original Introduction

Yan Tai[1] Daoist Fang, his age is unknown. People associated with him said that their grandfathers practiced together with him about 100 years ago. His voice is powerful like a bell, (he stands) 7 chi (feet) straight and solid, and he can stun you like an awl (sharp iron point). As a game he can use a long rope tied to his wrist and drag several tens of people behind him or he can pull and control over ten people in the front. He can use two fingers to hook two people and suspend them and raise them up like they are flying. A person chasing him can never reach him. He very often spontaneously goes to Tong Zhuo city for cakes (buns), walking for over 40 Li (Chinese miles) and coming back. The cakes are still hot when he returns. People call him Di Xian (Ground Immortal).

When I was young I had many diseases. I tried medicine, Daoyin, and anything that could cure my diseases. At last, I got to know Mr. Fang. I tested him by playing around and with some games. I won't describe it in detail. I begged for his prescription for getting rid of diseases. Mr. Fang says, "The cleverness of my Dao (way) is to cure without medicine. The principles of the body are easy and simple. It complies with the movement of fate. When Heaven complies with it, then its' movement is healthy. When humans comply with this, life is extended. It is not only for curing disease."

---

1   Yan Tai appears several times in the original text in relation to Daoist Fang. A literal translation would be "Swallow Platform". The only reference I was able to find for this name was that during the Warring States period, Emperor Yan Zhao (who ruled from 313-279 BC) built this as a place to receive worthy people summoned to the court. As this would have been close to two thousand years before Daoist Fang's time, I am not sure what it is referencing. My guess is that it might be an honorific or that it might be something else.

Speaking of the method of Rubbing the Abdomen, if you study its Dao in detail, Yin and Yang combine in a clever way. In it, you are pressing the middle section (abdomen) and following the instructions to practice. The disease will become gradually less. Later, I told my friends and family who are sick about this method. All tried it and received wonderful results.

Mr. Fang's method is marvelous and great. He is regarded as a Shen Xian (Spirit Immortal) among men and it is because of this (method). I don't dare keep this to myself as a secret. I wrote this with the explanation and pictures and want to spread this, so I will not waste what I received in my ordinary life and also to let people of the world receive longevity.

Open record of Mr Fang, in Xin An

Continued Introduction

When I was young I liked to practice martial exercises and training. All exercises that are beneficial to the tendon, bone, Qi, blood, I practiced them all. Even though it was only beneficial to the body, never the less I am already 71 years old and my ears, eyes, hands, and feet show no signs of aging. Every time I think about this, I am very happy. This is the fortune of being without disease. I never added the intention to protect the body, and still I have this happiness.

When I was 49, I was an established government official in the village. During the seasonal flooding time, I was running around busily and worried too much which caused insomnia. For over 20 years I sought medical prescriptions to cure it. But none were effective. Then I received Immortal Fang's plain and simple Longevity Method from Mr Ran's collection. In the morning and the evening with my whole Heart (mind), with closed eyes, and regulated breathing, I studied it and abided by its methods to complete the training of Xing and Ming (Nature and Life). Within 2 months it was like my disease was gone. Every night, after class, I was able to sleep through the night and the next day my vitality was bright and clear. After walking for 10 Li (Chinese miles) the power in my legs feels light and healthy. So, I wanted to make a book covering this method. I named this method Zi Zheng[2] and transcribed several books. I gave them to people that I knew who had consumption and accumulation without appetite. They all recovered. Because of this, people who sought the book became numerous. It was hard to write enough, so I re-wrote the original copy in detail and gave it to a lot of people. For people who are healthy or for people who are old without disease, receiving this can extend the years. For people with disease, they can recover quickly. In this world, in this year, to have the fortune of having no disease and extending the years, it is a delightful thing.

16th day of the second month of Autumn, the Yi Mao year of Yong Zheng (1723-1735) by Song Xinru

Published again by Zhu Tianfu, eleventh month of the lunar calendar, Geng Shen year of Xian Feng (1851-1861), in Yan Shan (Swallow Mountain)

---

2   Zi is the time from 11pm to 1 am (midnight). It is the most Yin time of the day. During this time of utmost Yin is when the True Yang is born. This shown in the Taiji Diagram where the dot of Yang (white) is contained in the section with the most Yin (black). Zheng means when the sun appears. The name Zi Zheng is referencing that at the time of the utmost Yin, Yang appears (the sun appears). The sun in Chinese is called Tai Yang (Great Yang).

12

Immortal Fang's Longevity Qigong

Rubbing the Abdomen

to Prevent Illness and Prolong Life

Exercise 1

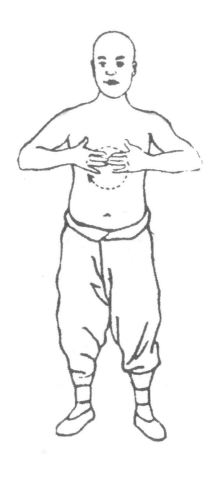

Close the eyes slightly,

Listen inward,

Breath evenly through the nose,

Close the mouth.

Use the middle three fingers of the two hands to press down at Xin Wo (pit or hollow of the heart – solar plexus).

From the left, going clockwise, lightly rub 21 times in a circle.

Exercise 2

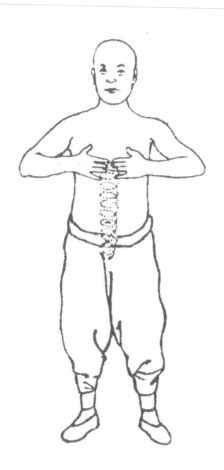

Rubbing is here,

Yi (Intention) is here,

Yin and Yang Combine,

The Winding Qi descends.

Use the middle three fingers of the two hands, from the Xin Wo (pit or hollow of the heart – solar plexus), to rub clockwise and go down.

As you rub, you move. Rub until below the umbilicus, to the height of the Gao Gu (pubic bone).

Exercise 3

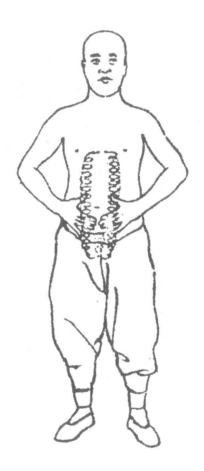

Jing (essence), Qi, and Shen (spirit)

can not govern themselves,

Learn to listen to the Yi (intention),

Yi (intention) moves, then you move.

Use the middle three fingers of the two hands, from the Gao Gu (pubic bone) area, to rub separately and ascend to the two sides.

As you rub, you move. Rub to the Xin Wo (pit or hollow of the heart – solar plexus), to where the two hands connect.

Exercise 4

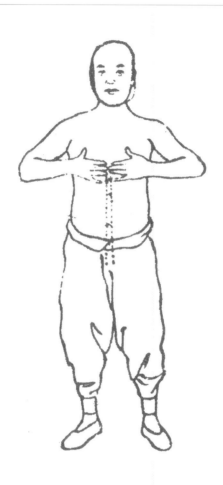

The left hand pushes down,

Down the Da Dong Mai (Aorta).

The right hand pushes down,

Down the Da Jing Mai (Vena Cava).

Use the middle three fingers of the two hands, from the Xin Wo (pit or hollow of the heart – solar plexus) area, to push straight down to the Gao Gu (pubic bone) 21 times.

Exercise 5

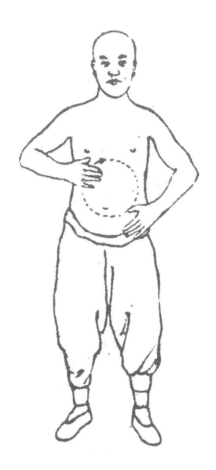

Circle and push left,

Diagonally on the stomach tendon.

Use the middle three fingers of the left hand to press where the leg clamps together and do not move.

Use the right hand to circle to the left and rub in a circle around the umbilicus 21 times.

Exercise 6

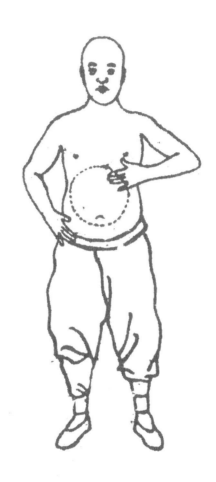

Circle and push right,

Diagonally on the stomach tendon.

Use the middle three fingers of the right hand to press where the leg clamps together and do not move.

Use the left hand to circle to the right and rub in a circle around the umbilicus 21 times.

Exercise 7

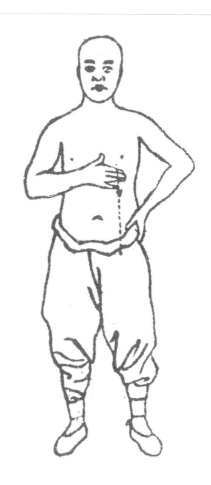

Straight pushing left,

Horizontally on the stomach tendon.

The left hand lightly pinches at the left side, on the soft part below the ribs, where the waist and the kidney are. The thumb is pointing forward and the four fingers are supporting the back.

Use the middle three fingers of the right hand, from the bottom of the left breast, to push straight down until where the leg clamps 21 times.

Exercise 8

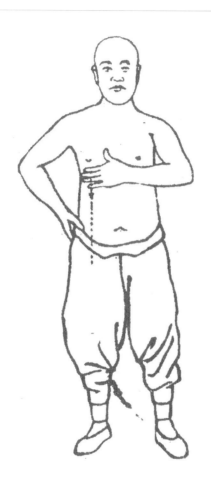

Straight pushing right,

Horizontally on the stomach tendon.

The right hand lightly pinches at the right side, on the soft part below the ribs, where the waist and the kidney are. The thumb is pointing forward and the four fingers are supporting the back.

Use the middle three fingers of the left hand, from the bottom of the right breast, to push straight down until where the leg clamps 21 times.

Exercise 9

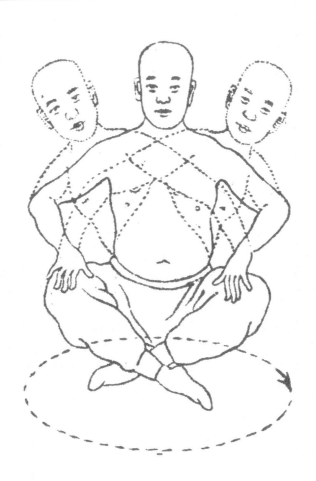

Sit and sway the bones of the whole body,

The joints are wrapped in Qi,

The Qi goes into the Spinal Marrow,

Up to the Cerebrum and Cerebellum,

Down to Qu Jiang (the abdomen),

It Fills the three Dan Tian,

and Opens the 100 Channels.

After the rubbing, sit down with the legs crossed. The middle three fingers of the two hands are on the knees. From the left to right, the right foot is on top and the left foot is on the bottom. Use a crossed (X) shape to bind the two feet. The tips of the fingers are slightly bent.

The chest and the shoulder crouch down in the posture of bowing two times. Then move from the front of the left knee and turn to the front of the right knee. Turn 21 times. Then as previously, turn from the right to the left 21 times.

In the previous method of Swaying the Body to the Left, the chest and shoulders sway out to the front of the left knee. Then sway to above the right knee. Then sway over the right knee towards the back and pull the waist back. It is best to sway and turn to the fullest. Do not sway quickly. Do not use strength.

How to Practice

There are two way to practice Rubbing the Abdomen. It can be divided into standing practice and lying down practice.

When standing up, the body is upright and straight. The neck appears vertical. The tongue to the roof of the mouth. The back must be rounded. The arms have to embrace. The tips of the shoulders must Kou (hook inward). The chest must be open and spread. The two shoulders must be relaxed. The lower abdomen drops down. The feet stand in the \ / shape posture. The heels must not be too far apart. The eyes look straight forward levelly. Continuously repeat (the sequence of exercises) 7 times and then stop. Then do the sitting according to picture 9 and rotate 21 times (each way).

For the lying down method, you must calm the Heart (quiet the mind) and calm the thoughts. The mattress needs to be level and the pillow needs to be short. Lie down on the back with the body straight. The feet are even and the toes are bent (relaxed naturally). Rub lightly and move slowly. Going through the exercises from 1 to 8, completing all the steps, counts as one. Every time you do the exercise, the breathing must be even, natural, seamless, and continuous.

Continuously repeat (the sequence of exercises) 7 times. Then sit up and sway 21 times (each way).

Practice this in the morning after you wake up, as a morning exercise, at noon, as noon exercise, and at night before you sleep, as a nighttime exercise. Do it three times a day normally. If you (have to) miss one (exercise session), miss the noon exercise. If you are busy, the morning and night exercise can not be missed.

In the beginning do the sequence of exercises (1 through 8) for 3 repetitions. After 3 days, do 5 repetitions. After 3 day, do 7 repetitions. No matter if you are a man or a woman, it is suitable for all people, except for pregnant women who are forbidden (to practice).

Explanation of the Complete Practice

This method follows the intrinsic order, in every possible way, of the mechanism of generation and change (the endless cosmic force of creation and transformation). It is easy to see. The root of Heaven and Earth is Yin and Yang. Yin and Yang govern movement and stillness. The human body is Yin and Yang. Yin and Yang is movement and stillness. When movement and stillness combine in harmony, Qi and blood are harmonious and unimpeded. All kinds of diseases and ailments are not generated. Only then can you complete your natural span of life.

If you are led by sexual passion or lust, then you will always violate movement and stillness. Too much movement damages the Yin, and there must be a prevalence of Yang. Too much stillness damages the Yang, and there must be a prevalence of Yin. If Yin is damaged and Yang has not fully developed, then Yang is also damaged. If Yang is damaged and Yin has not generated, then Yin is also damaged. (When Yin or Yang is) already damaged, the mechanism of generation and change (the endless cosmic force of creation and transformation) has already stopped working. If you don't have a way to guide it, the source of generating and transforming can not be restarted.

This method of Rubbing the Abdomen uses movement to transform stillness and stillness to facilitate movement. It conforms with Yin and Yang. It complies with the Five Elements, their mechanism of generation and the spirit of their changes. That is why it can connect and harmonize the top and bottom, put Yin and Yang back in order, get rid of the old and generate the new, replenish the five internal organs (Heart, Liver, Spleen, Lungs, and Kidneys), expel all the externally contracted evils, and get rid of all kinds of internally generated diseases and ailments. It supplements deficiency and drains excess. This method of dispersing and strengthening has infinite wonderful results. Why use medicines and elixirs when you have actual results of preventing illness and prolonging life (without them)?

Postscript

This is Yan Tai Daoist Fang's oral teaching on the Rubbing the Abdomen Method. It was written in Yongzheng (1723-1735) at the royal court of Xin An. It had an Introduction and Illustrations. The records were published and given to the world. There are pictures of the nine methods. It is easy and simple.

Government Official Peng and I wrote about receiving the benefits of Yang Sheng (Nourishing Life). I do not keep this secret to myself. I told it to Mr Lu Yisu. Yisu received it and published it and gave it to the world. That is what the intention of a benevolent gentleman should be.

Uneducated people say that poverty and wealth and high or low status is dictated by the Heavens. Actually, you should seek health, strength, peace, and happiness your self. If you are not strong and healthy, then 10,000 diseases will be generated. Even if you are rich, how can you be happy? If you can be healthy and strong, then you will be full of Jing (essence) and Li (strength). Even if you are poor, you will not have difficulty in your work. That is why strong and healthy people are the mother of peace and happiness.

Government Official Peng and I were officials in Hubei province. Now I am 77 and in Shanghai. My health is still the same. Yisu and I work together at the head office of Steamship Investments. Even though we work all day bent over a table conducting business, our Qi is not stagnant and our vitality and spirit is lively and happy. Our faces are glowing and flourishing. These are the signs of health, strength, and happiness. This is the result of what is written.

First month of the lunar year, year Bing Yin (1926), combined the books into a slip case and reprinted it, wrote a few words to entertain people with the same interests

Wu Heshou, start of the rainy season, year 64, in Wu Jin

Original Chinese Edition

僕體素羸弱，魚有肺病，時止時發，醫
藥兩窮，諗形意拳可療此病思練習
之，適靳君雲亭自都南下鳳檀此術，
相與討論行之數年，所患若失，因高
靳君將所藏形意拳秘本付刊，冀有

以療與吾同病者，已付大東書局印

其譜與圖說矣，乃聲相應而氣相求，

武進戚我彭觀察善養生，鶴髮童顏，

神采弈弈，今春授以此本，曰余今年

七十有六，體質猶健者，習此攄數十

寒暑未嘗間斷耳，君同志也，以此相

贈，僕辰閱一遍多屬却病之法与形意
拳不類而頴茲獲其生機神其變化以
動化靜以靜運動似較形意拳尤為妥
逸也惟此書始於雍正續於咸豐原板
今已無存，如廣陵散矣特与靳君細加
泰考暑為俗正付諸石印以公同好至

爵行十法詳載圖說茲不復贅云

歲次乙丑仲冬月上澣

京兆霸縣呂一素識

原序

燕臺方道者不知紀年，偕之遊者輒
言與其祖父相習約近百年人物也多
功聲如鐘，七尺挺壓撼之磊鐵戲者以
長繩繫其腕令十數人拽之後引手
十餘人譽而前以三指鈎二人懸而

起行如飛，追逐者莫能及。常一刻往通州市餅，行四十餘里歸，餅猶炙手人。皆稱為地仙。云余少多疾，藥餌導引，凡可愈疾者無不徧訪，最後始識方君元遊戲玩弄之術，試其技能者不具述。第求其却病之方，方君曰：吾道

之妙，醫不假藥，體乎易簡之理，合乎
運行之戲，天以是而健行人以是而
延生，豈第却病已乎，乃語以摩腹一
法，細推其道，妙合陰陽中按節度余
循習行之疾累漸減，後以此法語親
友中病者，無不試有奇效，即方君之

瑰奇偉異，目為神仙中人者亦率由

此，余不敢自祕，續其圖說，付之剞劂，

以廣其傳。既不昧平生之所得力，亦

欲世人共登壽域云爾。

　　　　　新安方開錄

續序

余幼年好武喜操練，凡有益於筋骨
氣血者，無不習之，雖為軀殼起見，然
年已七十有一，耳目手足卒無衰老
之狀，每一思之，快然自足曰此無病
之福也，向非加意保身，安能有此樂

哉，惟於四十九歲官樹村汛時奔走勞心太甚致患失眠，迄今二十餘年徧訪醫方調治，竟未能愈，茲得樸之舟公所藏方仙延年法，朝夕定心閉目調息守中如法課之，作為性命之工，未及兩月憊已若失，每晚課畢竟能徹夜酣

睡，次日精神奕朗，行數十里腳力更

覺輕健於是將此法命子聶鈔錄數

冊傳與素識之患虛癆及停飲者無

不愈，由是索取者日繁，筆墨難於應

付即將原本重為繕寫詳校付梓以

廣其傳俾壯老無病者獲此可以延

年有病者即可速愈舉斯世盡延年

無病之福豈非大快事耶

雍正乙卯仲秋既望

咸豐歲次庚申冬月

燕山宋炘如珠田甫重刊

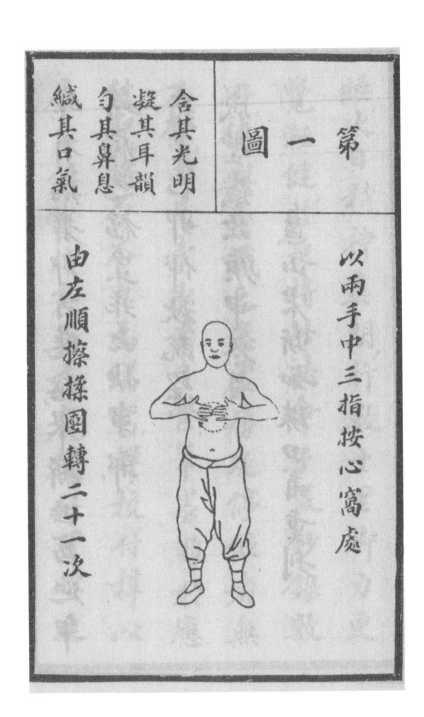

第一圖

緘其口氣
白其鼻息
凝其耳韻
含其光明

由左順擦揉圓轉二十一次

以兩手中三指按心窩處

50

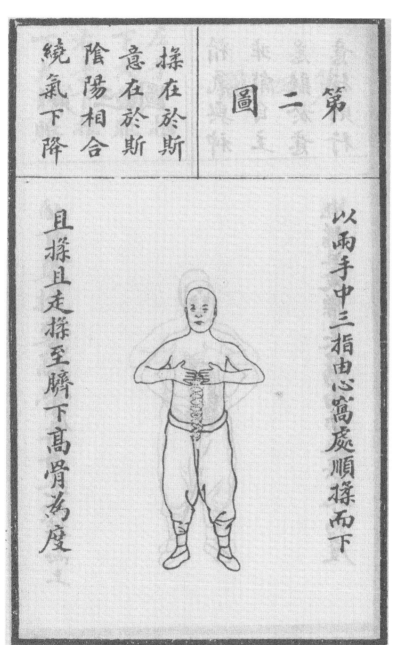

第二圖

操在於斯
意在於斯
陰陽相合
繞氣下降

以兩手中三指由心窩處順操而下

且操且走操至臍下高骨為度

51

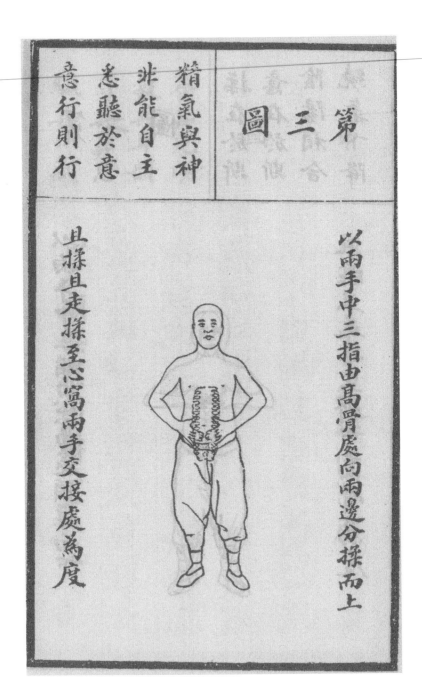

第三圖

精氣與神
非能自主
悉聽於意
意行則行

以兩手中三指由高骨處向兩邊分揉而上

且揉且走揉至心窩兩手交接處為度

52

左手下推
下大動脈
右手下推
下大靜脈

以兩手中三指由心窩處

向下直推至高骨二十一次

53

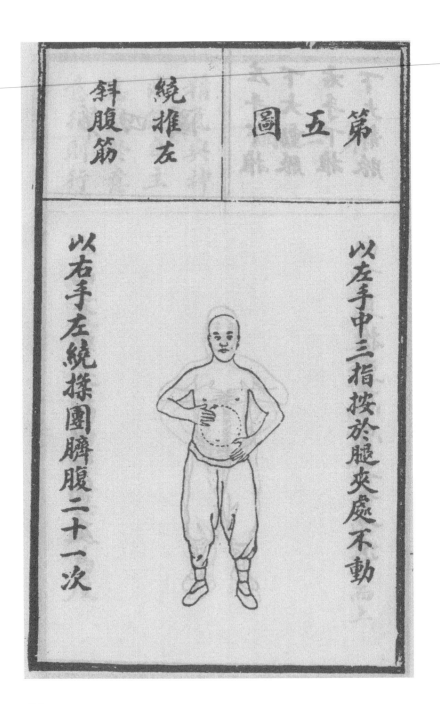

第五圖

繞推左
斜腹筋

以左手中三指按於腿夾處不動

以右手左繞揉團臍腹二十一次

54

第六圖

繞推右

斜腹筋

以右手中三指按於腿夾處不動

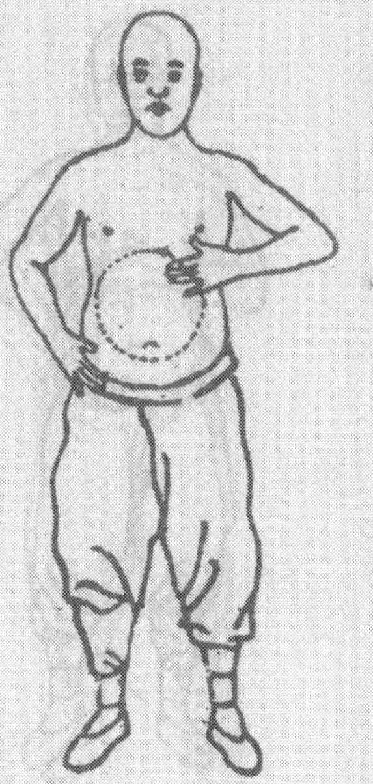

以左手右繞揉團臍腹二十一次

55

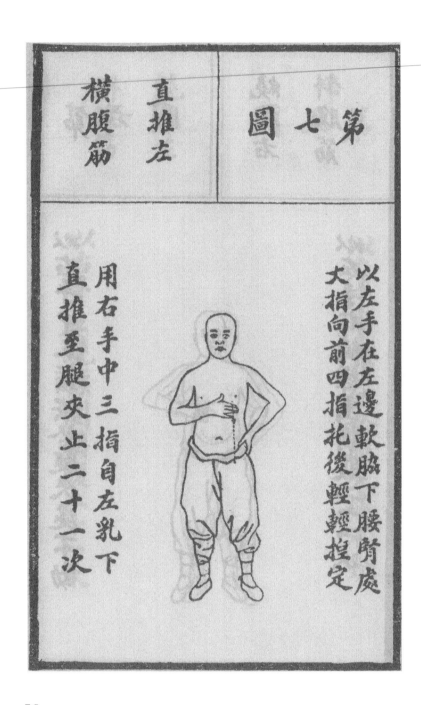

第七圖

直推左

橫腹筋

以左手在左邊軟脅下腰臀處大指向前四指托後輕輕捏定

用右手中三指自左乳下直推至腿夾止二十一次

56

直推右

橫腹筋

以右手在右邊軟脅下腰腎處
大指向前四指托後輕輕捏定

用左手中三指自右乳下
直推至腿夾止二十一次

57

坐搖周身骨

骼骨節帶氣

氣道荷髓上

至夫腦小腦

下達曲江灘

三田道百脈

搋搓畢趺坐以兩手中三指按兩膝上由左往右

右足在上左足在下以十字絞兩足十指似稍鉤曲

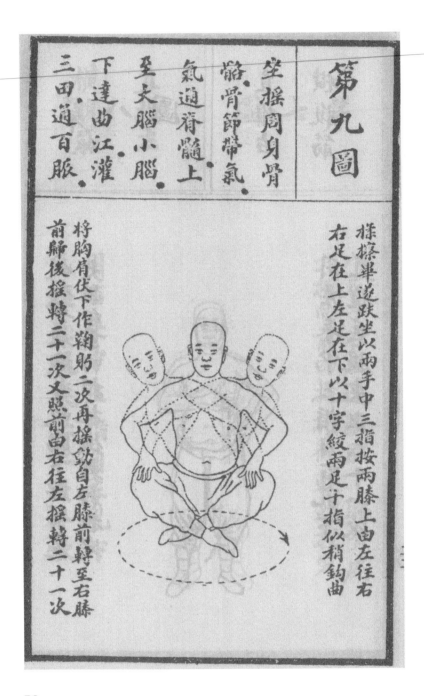

將胸肯伏下作鞠躬二次再搖訖自右膝前轉至右膝

前歸後搖轉二十一次又照前由右往左搖轉二十一次

前法如搖身向左，即將胸肩搖出左
膝前向，即搖伏膝上，向右即搖出右
膝向後，即弓腰後撒，總以搖轉滿足
為妙，不可急搖，俱使著力

59

揉腹可分立功卧功兩法，立功身宜

正直，項有豎相，舌頂上膛，脊背要圓

臂肘要抱膀尖要扣胸膛開展，兩肩

要鬆，小腹下垂，脚立八字，趾跟相離

不可太遠，目向前視以平為度，連做

七度畢即按照第九圖趺坐揉轉二

十一次。卧功須息心靜慮，宜平席矮枕，正身仰卧齊足，屈指輕摩緩動，將八圖挨次做完為一度，每逢做時呼吸平勻，純任自然循環無端，綿綿不斷，連做七度畢，即起坐摩轉二十一次，照此清晨睡醒時做為早課，午中

做為午課,晚來臨睡做為晚課,日以
三課為常,倘遇有事,早晚兩課必不
可少,初做時一課三度,三日後一課
五度,再三日後一課七度,無論男婦
皆宜,惟孕者忌之。

全圖說

全圖則理備生化之機更易見也天
地本乎陰陽陰陽主乎動靜人身一
陰陽也陰陽一動靜也動靜合宜氣
血和暢百病不生乃得盡其天年如
為情欲所牽永違動靜過動傷陰陽

必偏勝過靜傷陽陰必偏朦且陰傷

而陽無所成陽亦傷也陽傷而陰無

所生陰血傷也既傷矣生之變化之

機已寨非用法以導之則生化之源

亦曲磋也揉腹之法以動化靜以靜

運動合乎陰陽順乎五行發其生機

神其變化，故能通和上下，分理陰陽，去舊生新充實五臟驅外感之諸邪，消內生之百痾補不足瀉有餘消長之道妙應無窮何須藉藥燒丹自有卻病延年之實效耳。

是編為燕臺方道口授探腹法清雍正

朝新安方開績具圖說，刊行世圖九

九法簡而逸，同邑盛我彭觀察之養生

得力是編不自秘以授呂君一素，一素

復得力是編不自秘期公諸世，皆仁人

之用心也，愚謂人生貧富貴賤聽諸天，

康強安樂求諸己不康強則百病叢生，

雖富貴何樂能康強則精力充實雖

貧賤而翔業非難故康強者安樂之

母世我彭觀察叢與余同仕鄂令寓

滬年七十有七健康猶首一素与余共

事輪船招商總局竟日伏案治事氣不

惰且精神愉快容采煥發皆康強安
樂之徵求即得力是編之效丙寅春正
月一素屬書全帙將付石印爰綴數語
於後以餉同志云

武進吳鶴守繹甫時年六十有四

About the Translator

Franklin Fick is a long time practitioner and teacher of Traditional Chinese Kung Fu, Qigong, Meditation, and Healing Arts. He also has a Masters Degree in Acupuncture and Traditional Chinese Medicine.

Sifu Fick has been offering Online Lessons since 2010. For more information please visit:

spiritdragoninstitute.com

About Shen Long Publishing

Franklin founded Shen Long publishing in 2005 with the goal to provide the best information and learning materials related to: Traditional Chinese Martial Arts, Qigong, Meditation, and Traditional Healing.

For a complete listing of our products please visit Shen Long Publishing's website at:

shenlongpub.com

56304536R00043

Made in the USA
Columbia, SC
23 April 2019